THE INTRUDER

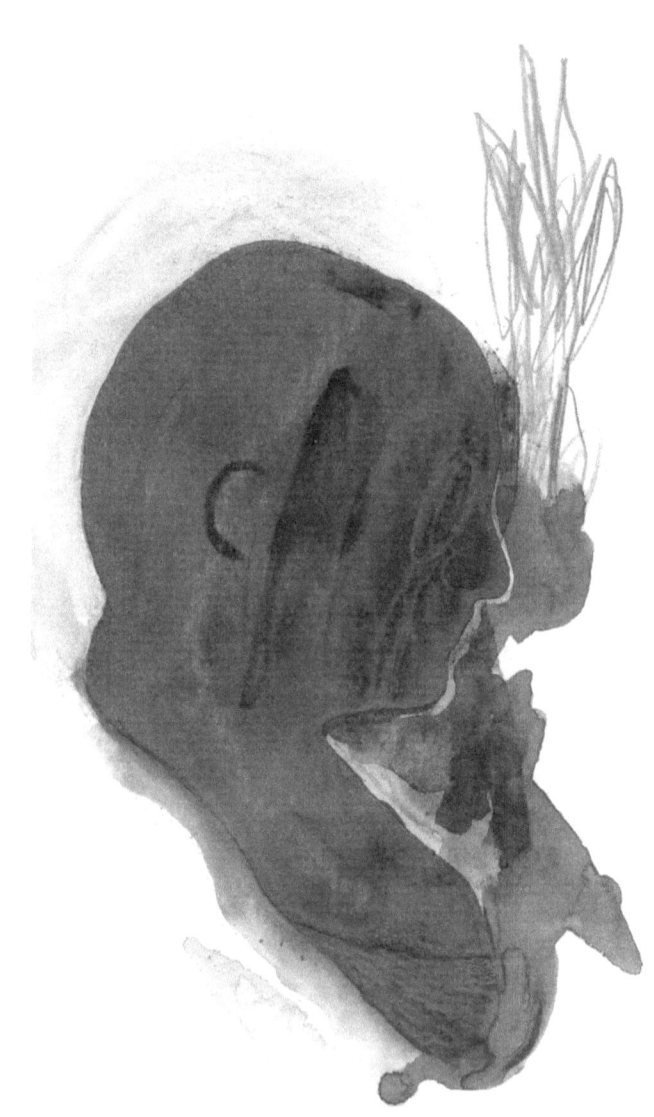

The Intruder

Jean-Luc Nancy

*Translated by Richard Rand,
Jeff Fort, and Anna Moschovakis*
Introduction by Jeff Fort
Foreword by Claire Denis

FORDHAM UNIVERSITY PRESS   NEW YORK 2024

Copyright © 2024 Fordham University Press

This book was originally published in French as Jean-Luc Nancy, *L'intrus*, Copyright © Éditions Galilée, 2000–2017.

Frontispiece: François Martin

All rights reserved. No part of this publication may be reproduced, stored in a retrieval system, or transmitted in any form or by any means—electronic, mechanical, photocopy, recording, or any other—except for brief quotations in printed reviews, without the prior permission of the publisher.

Fordham University Press has no responsibility for the persistence or accuracy of URLs for external or third-party Internet websites referred to in this publication and does not guarantee that any content on such websites is, or will remain, accurate or appropriate.

Fordham University Press also publishes its books in a variety of electronic formats. Some content that appears in print may not be available in electronic books.

Visit us online at www.fordhampress.com.

Library of Congress Cataloging-in-Publication Data available online at https://catalog.loc.gov.

Printed in the United States of America
26 25 24   5 4 3 2 1
First edition

Contents

FOREWORD
Claire Denis ix

Introduction
Jeff Fort 1

The Intruder 9

Toward Nancy 47

The Intruder according to Claire Denis 57

THE INTRUDER

Foreword
by Claire Denis

Something happened in France in the mid-90s—the question of borders. People felt—and still feel—that there was a big problem of crossing the border illegally. There arose a large movement in France and elsewhere in Europe against these border crossings, and at the same time a movement in favor of opening borders.

It's very hard and very strange to live by a place that is closed. So in 1996 in France, a movement began among filmmakers, and it created a movement with a lot of other people—unions, lawyers, doctors—against the idea that a supposedly newly opened Europe would be closed because the people who wanted to come in were poor. It started with interviews in newspapers and moved to protests.

Around that time, the philosopher Jacques Derrida wrote a book called *Of Hospitality*. Derrida asked another French philosopher, a friend of his, Jean-Luc Nancy, to also write a piece about borders.[1] Jean-Luc had been very sick—he had had a heart transplant a few years before. He had never written or spoken about that topic as a philosopher. But now he took up this provocation in a surprising way. He wrote a short book—is it a meditation? a novel? called *L'intrus—The Intruder*—about his heart transplant. He compared the intrusion into his body to the intrusion across a border. And he said, in a way, you cannot intrude without a certain violence. If it's soft, it's not an intrusion. Intrusion has to be brutal. Otherwise, it's not an intrusion anymore. For people who want to cross the border, it's also brutal.

When I read this book, I was in the middle of shooting a film called *Trouble Every Day*. Jean-Luc's book is very short; I read it overnight. It somehow articulated both this feeling of having in his chest the heart of someone he doesn't know, and people trespassing borders. Jean-Luc remembered noticing in the hospital that it was mainly men who received transplants. With women it was much more rare. But these men kept asking the surgeon: "Of course, I want a new heart to survive, but not a woman's heart, please. A man, a male heart, not a female heart, please." And an extra demand: "And not from a Black person."

When I decided I had to film *The Intruder*, I started to write the script as if I were translating Jean-Luc's book. He told me: "Although it's from me, it's not my book." I said, "Yes, it's your book. In my vision, in a way, it's your book. It's about a man who is selfish enough, who wants to buy a new heart and not pay the debt." Jean-Luc was very close to me. And he told me: "You never did an adaptation of the book. You adopted it. That's different."

This film was made with a spirit of freedom, despite the fact that we had almost no money. We started shooting in France, then crossed the border to Switzerland. I chose a place in France, an area called the Jura, a place that really exists. It's not a province, it exists almost defined by the border with Switzerland, because the Jura is a poor area, and

Switzerland is rich. Many people cross the border to work in Switzerland. I was attracted by that.

There was also this sense that in Switzerland you could make strange deals, like buying clandestine organs. You can still see this on the internet today. When I started thinking about this, I thought, well, the world is round, and maybe this guy is going to go to the South Pacific as if he were following the curve of the surface of Earth—going to the Southern Hemisphere, because he lived in a cold country.

And there in the Southern Hemisphere, he's like Robert Louis Stevenson. He's like Gauguin, thinking that in the South Pacific, everything is great, like in the musical. Every moment is fantastic—a paradise for people from the North. Of course it's fake. I took this trip in my mind, and the film is taking it also, like a loop.

I thought for a long time about whether I would shoot a heart transplant for real. If you've seen the movie *Vice* (which didn't exist then), you've seen a heart transplant surgery. But I went to the hospital and was invited to see one. And I thought, no, it's not proper for a film to show that. Maybe I should instead create this strange ellipsis for a new man with a new heart. Maybe I was wrong. Anyway, with this new heart, this guy is missing the most important thing, something that really belongs to him. Not his whole heart, this heart that doesn't function anymore, but his own life.

Introduction
Jeff Fort

> I was already no longer in me.
> —JEAN-LUC NANCY, *THE INTRUDER*

In the year 2000, Jean-Luc Nancy, a philosopher with a long list of works already behind him, published an unusual book, which he titled *L'intrus, The Intruder*. Having been asked to write something on the question of the stranger, the foreigner who arrives, he was no doubt inevitably drawn to an extremely intimate form of strangeness with which— thanks to which—he had been living for years. Put simply, his heart gave out, and he had to have another, or another's, that of an unknown person, grafted into his body. This transplant, which took place in 1991, was one of the first carried out in France, and it gave Nancy thirty more years of life. It also revealed to him, in a more visceral way than most of us ever experience, the strangeness of bodily existence and the radical otherness that inhabits and makes possible every self and every sensing body. This essay, something of an intrusive presence in Nancy's already diverse body of work, combines philosophical reflection and first-person experience. It grapples with an extraordinarily complex and precarious physical balance between external medical interventions and autoimmune responses, as the immunosuppressant drugs required for the body's acceptance of this foreign organ caused a cancer that had to be treated as well. The unlikely passage through the years became narrow and cumbersome to manage (though by all accounts he bore it lightly, even cheerfully). As Nancy writes, quoting a doctor involved in these many technical and pharmacological ministrations, his body became a kind of factory in need of constant careful oversight. Fortunately for readers of Nancy, this keen awareness seems only to have enhanced the production and depth of his remarkable texts. But only here in *The Intruder* does he describe the dizzying conditions under which that production occurred, indicating the unsettling perspectives that this experience opened, quite literally, in and through a body becoming obtrusively other to itself.

This translation of *The Intruder* includes three substantial postscripts not included in the original publication, which are translated here for the first time. These were added to successive editions of the work until it reached its definitive form in a *nouvelle édition augmentée* published by Éditions Galilée in 2017. Nancy died in August 2021 at the age of eighty-one. These postscripts thus mark out the scansion of an ongoing but uncertain survival, both cautiously celebrating anniversaries and worrying how much longer he might continue. They show him puzzling over the unsettling arbitrariness of his own continued existence, meditating on the technical mediations in which it remained inextricably entangled, and acknowledging the absence of friends who have passed in the meantime. And yet, Nancy implies, I who had no right to go on living, I remain.

The Intruder is also the strange name of a strange film that Nancy's friend Claire Denis released in 2004 and that was voted one of the two hundred fifty greatest films of all time in *Sight and Sound*'s 2023 poll of critics from around the world. That film ends with the following intertitle, which appears just after its final images: "The book by Jean-Luc Nancy, *The Intruder*, was an inspiration for the film." (Oddly, it does not say "for this film," as though something more general, more exterior, were already at issue as the end credits begin to roll.) This is not the place for a commentary on the relation between the book and the movie, which remains enigmatic, fragmentary, more evocative than thematic, a matter of intersecting threads in a loose weave, or perhaps an overlapping but divergent pattern of scars.[1] Indeed Nancy himself, in the dense essay on the film included here, refrains from commenting on the relationship between the book and the film, which he calls "a secret" known only to its director. That essay, "*The Intruder* According to Claire Denis," focuses instead on the symbolic, visual, and corporeal "strands" running through the film's elliptical narrative. At its core, Denis's film does involve a heart transplant, and it takes place in an atmosphere of menacing encroachments and bodily transgressions, a fraying sense of autonomy in a world of porous borders anxiously guarded. Martine Beugnet nicely formulates one schematic point of convergence, in terms that apply to both Nancy's text and Denis's projective recasting: "Nancy explores how the experience of one's identity being threatened from within by that which comes from the outside is complicated by the need to lower one's defenses, to weaken one's immune system in order to survive."[2] In other words, the experience of intrusion is necessarily one of exposure and risk, such that survival can be threatened not only by a dangerous outsider but also, and conversely, by a desire for total immunity at all costs, a drive to rigidify borders, when strangeness is met with the violent panic of expulsion.

At another level, we could say that an openness to contagion, and to transplantation—this intrusion in kind into the body's "montage of functions" as Nancy puts it—is endemic to cinema itself, which always absorbs its material from the world it photographs and from the forms and elements of previous films. In this case, Denis's "intruder" is played by Michel Subor, who comes into this film with the weight of a previous role from decades earlier, in Jean-Luc Godard's *Le petit soldat* (1963), shot in 1960 during the Algerian War of Independence but banned until the war was over. He also brings with him a cinematic memory of Tahiti (where the final segment of *The Intruder* takes place), which Denis splices in from yet another earlier film, implying that it belongs to her character's past: the unfinished *Le reflux* (1965), by Paul Gégauff (a right-wing anarchist friend of Godard's), which names in its title the "ebb tide" that draws these cinematic references into a multilayered resonance of filmic and historic time. If one can speak of Denis "transplanting *L'intrus* to the screen,"[3] it is partly by way of such Frankensteinian constructions, through which a body survives in the scarred montage of its still moving images.[4]

A third text included here consists of an edited transcription of a short film that Denis made with Nancy before filming *The Intruder*. "Toward Nancy" was released in 2002 as part of an omnibus collection of shorts called *Ten Minutes Older: The Cello*, which, along with its companion film (*Ten Minutes Older: The Trumpet*), pays homage to Herz Frank's 1978 short "Ten Minutes Older" and includes fifteen films by a remarkable roster of cinematic luminaries. Jean-Luc Godard is a strange presence here as well, and not only because he contributed to the series. Denis's contribution is itself an homage, indeed a direct citation and restaging, of a twelve-minute-long sequence from Godard's *La Chinoise* (1967), a sequence marked off there with an intertitle: "Encounter with Francis Jeanson." Jeanson was a philosopher, writer, editor, and left-wing political activist who had fought with the French Liberation Army at the end of World War II and later became a well-known dissident during the Algerian War of Independence, when he was arrested and jailed by French authorities for organized activities in support of the anticolonial Front de Libération Nationale in Algeria. In Godard's film, Jeanson plays himself just as Nancy does here. Confronting Jeanson with the militant language dissected throughout Godard's film, Véronique (Anne Wiazemsky), a revolutionary university student sporting a Mao-style hat, engages in a heated debate with the older man regarding the nature of revolutionary action, as they sit in a train compartment in the same configuration as Nancy and the young woman in Denis's film (played by Ana Samardzija). Nancy's interlocutor, for her part, is much less confrontational, and her inquisitive demeanor might also remind one of the conversation between Anna Karina and the philosopher Brice Parain in another film by Godard, *Vivre sa vie* (1962). (I note in passing the curious repetition of these names: Anna, Anne, Ana . . .).

The title *Toward Nancy* refers not just to the philosopher's name but also to the city of Nancy, which lies about halfway between Paris and Strasbourg, the Alsatian city where Nancy lived and worked for many decades. Depending on the direction of the journey, this title might be read differently (in terms of screen direction, the landscape moves left to right, which feels like westward movement, the opposite of Godard's); either way, it refers to a smaller town between cities that are well known in the broader European context (Strasbourg being one of the two alternating seats of the European Parliament). Nancy is a less cosmopolitan town and one that is located more deeply within *la France profonde* (a bit like "middle America"), and it represents a movement into a more provincial (also whiter) social space where the question of the stranger and the foreigner might play out in somewhat starker fashion than in either of the major cities on opposite ends of the train line. This "between" or "middle" space is underscored as such by several shots through the window of the rapid train, which was designed to pass through these landscapes as quickly as possible.

The broader ideological problems addressed in the dialogue, however, are central to and pervasive within French society and politics at large. Nancy's comments and the young woman's dilemma as a foreigner in France appear against the background of a universalist French Republican tradition that demands assimilation—including a supposed color-blindness with respect to race and ethnicity and a (selective) refusal of religious adherence in the public sphere. Denis's wandering camera moves from the conversing pair to an unknown man outside their space (played by Alex Descas, a well-known French actor of Caribbean descent who has acted in several of Denis's films), shifting its distance from longer shots to close-ups, and again to views of the landscape through the train's window. This spatial fragmentation offers a social dynamism absent from Godard's more compartmentalized encounter.

At the end of the film, Descas enters the train compartment occupied by Nancy and Samardzija and takes a seat. In this context, where a Black man interrupts, intrudes upon, and enters as a stranger into the enclosed space of a conversation between two white characters—a staged encounter that might be seen as too deliberately overdetermined in its message—it is important to stress once again a very significant point. When Nancy speaks of strangeness and the stranger, and of an irreducible intrusive otherness, the point is not to "other" anyone who happens to arrive from some elsewhere, or who has long since been there, but to insist first of all on a fundamental otherness "in" any "self," and thus on the necessity of reckoning with an inevitable internal otherness, a built-in fragmentation of the "proper"—which means likewise reckoning with the irreducible strangeness of any "other" at all, however intimate or distant they may be. It is in this sense that a blind and rigid demand for assimilation into sameness can only come up against the harsh dangers of autoimmune refusal, the violent denial of singularities and of the multiplicity of what *one* is.

"I was no longer in me": Nancy's simple formula states a truth that threatens every border with a knowledge of its illusory rigidity and the false homogeneity of what it would protect. Ultimately, Nancy tells us with unsettling lucidity, everybody—every body—is an intruder *of itself*, even as the otherness no one can live without risks being "assimilated" into ever expanding and potentially uncontrollable systems of technical mediation. It is no coincidence that the drive to homogeneity gives rise to these very systems, whether at border checkpoints or in the melee of cultural politics and economic triage, a fact that only intensifies the need to navigate these dangers, as Nancy strove to do, with courage and "with an open heart," as one so aptly says, whoever it may be.

A note on the translation: The irreducible otherness at issue in this work applies of course to languages as well. As though to prove the point with an especially relevant set of words, the French *étranger* and its cognates present a particular difficulty in English, where *étranger* can be rendered either as *stranger* or as *foreigner*, terms that resonate in an overlapping but very distinct set of connotations. I have often chosen to include both, while also hoping not to overburden the syntax, particularly in the spoken language of "Toward Nancy." That text retains certain aspects of this spoken style, but numerous small repetitions and hesitations have been removed for the sake of fluidity. While the translation is more complete and literal than film subtitles can be, in some instances I took a cue from the fine subtitles included in the DVD. I would like to thank Rob Hether for a very detailed transcription of the film's dialogue. I would also like to thank Tom Lay at Fordham University Press for his customary editorial acumen and his indispensable work in conceiving and shaping this volume.

The Intruder

There is in fact nothing so ignobly useless and superfluous as the organ called the heart, the filthiest invention that beings could have invented for pumping me with life.

—ANTONIN ARTAUD

The intruder introduces himself forcefully, by surprise or by ruse, not, in any case, by right or by being admitted beforehand. Something of the stranger has to intrude, or else he loses his strangeness.[1] If he already has the right to enter and stay, if he is awaited and received, no part of him being unexpected or unwelcome, then he is not an intruder anymore, but then neither is he any longer a stranger. To exclude all intrusiveness from the stranger's coming is therefore neither logically acceptable nor ethically admissible.

If, once he is there, he remains a stranger, then for as long as this remains so—and does not simply become "naturalized"—his coming does not stop: He continues to come, and his coming does not stop intruding in some way: in other words, without right or familiarity, not according to custom, being, on the contrary, a disturbance, a trouble in the midst of intimacy.

We have to think this through, and therefore to put it into practice: Otherwise the strangeness of the stranger would be reabsorbed—it would no longer be an issue—before he even crossed the threshold. To welcome a stranger, moreover, is necessarily to experience his intrusion. For the most part, we would rather not admit this: The very theme of the intruder intrudes upon our moral correctness (and is in fact a remarkable example of the *politically correct*).[2] But it is inseparable from the stranger's truth. This moral correctness presupposes that, upon receiving the stranger, we efface his strangeness at the threshold: It aims thereby not to have received him at all. But the stranger insists and intrudes. This fact is hard to receive, and perhaps to conceive . . .

I (who, "I"? this is precisely the question, an old question: Who is the subject of this utterance, ever alien to the subject of its statement, whose intruder it certainly is, though certainly also its motor, its shifter, or its heart)—I, then, received someone else's heart, about ten years ago. It was grafted into me. My own [*propre*] heart (you will have understood that this is the whole question of the "proper"—or else it is nothing of the sort, and then there is properly nothing to understand, no mystery, not even a question: just the simple fact of a transplant, as the doctors prefer to call it)—my own heart, then, was useless, for reasons never explained. In order, therefore, to live, I had to receive the heart of another person.

(But what other program, then, was intersecting with my physiological program? Less than twenty years earlier, no one was doing grafts, and certainly not protecting against their rejection through the use of cyclosporin. Twenty years hence, to be sure, other grafts will involve other methods. Personal contingency intersects with the contingency of technological history. Earlier I would be dead, later I would survive by other means. But "I" always finds itself tightly squeezed in a wedge of technical possibilities. Hence the vain debate, as I watched it unfold, between those who wanted to consider it a metaphysical adventure and those who saw it as a technical performance: Certainly both are at stake, each inside the other.)

After they told me I needed a graft, any sign could fluctuate, any data be reversed. Without further reflection, certainly, without even identifying an act, a permutation. Just the physical sensation of a void already opened up in the chest, a sort of apnea where nothing, absolutely nothing, even today, could help me disentangle the organic from the symbolic and imaginary, or what was continuous from what was interrupted: It was like a single gasp, exhaled thereafter through a strange cavern already imperceptibly opened up and like the spectacle, indeed, of leaping overboard while staying up on the bridge.

If my own heart was failing me, to what degree was it "mine," my "own" organ? Was it even an organ? For some years I had already felt a fluttering, some breaks in the rhythm, really not much of anything (mechanical figures, like the "ejection fraction," whose name I liked): not an organ, not the dark red muscular mass loaded with tubes that I now had to suddenly imagine. Not "my heart" beating endlessly, hitherto as absent as the soles of my feet while walking.

It became strange to me, intruding by defection: almost by rejection, if not by dejection. I had this heart at the tip of my tongue, like improper food. Rather like heartburn, but gently. A gentle sliding separated me from myself. I was there, it was summertime, we had to wait, something broke away from me, or this thing surged up inside me, where nothing had been before: nothing but the "proper" immersion inside me of a "myself" never identified as this body, still less as this heart, suddenly watching itself. Later on, for example, when climbing stairs, feeling each release of an "extrasystole" like the falling of a pebble to the bottom of a well. How do you become a representation to yourself? And a montage of functions? And where, then, does it go, that potent, silent evidence that was holding things together so uneventfully?

My heart became my stranger: strange precisely because it was inside. The strangeness could come from outside only because it surged up first on the inside. What a void suddenly opened up in the chest or the soul—they're one and the same—as soon as I was told: "You will need a transplant" . . . Here, the mind pushes against nothing: nothing to know, nothing to understand, nothing to sense. The intrusion of a body foreign to thought. This blank will stay with me like thought itself and its contrary, at one and the same time.

A heart that only half beats is only half my heart. I was already no longer in me. I'm already coming from somewhere else, or I'm not coming any longer at all. A strangeness is revealed "at the heart" of the most familiar—but "familiar" hardly says it: at the heart of something that never signaled itself as "heart." Up to this point, it was strange by virtue of not being even perceptible, not even being present. From now on it fails, and this strangeness binds me to myself. "I" am, because I am ill. ("Ill" is not exactly the term: not infected, just rusty, tight, blocked.) But this other, my heart, is done for. This heart, from now on intrusive, has to be extruded.

No doubt this can only happen if I want it, along with several others. "Several others": those who are close to me, but also the doctors, and, finally, myself, now doubled or multiplied more than ever before. Always for different motives, this whole world has to agree, in unison, to believe that prolonging my life is worth the effort. It isn't hard to picture the complexity of this strange group, intervening thus in the most sensitive part of "me." Let's pass over those who are close and pass over my-"self" (which, however, as I have said, is doubled: A strange suspension of judgment makes me picture myself as dying without protest, but also without attraction . . . we feel the heart weakening, we think we are going to die, we feel that we aren't going to feel anything anymore). But the doctors—here a whole team—are far more involved than I might have supposed: They have to decide, first of all, on whether a graft is indicated, then propose it without imposing it. (In doing so, they tell me there's to be a constraining "follow-up," nothing more—and what else could they guarantee? Eight years later, and after many other problems, I will develop a cancer brought on by the treatment, but today I'm still alive; who knows what's "worth the trouble," and what trouble?)

But the doctors also have to decide, as I will learn bit by bit, on inscription in a waiting list (in my case, for example, to accede to my demand not to be scheduled before the end of summer: presuming a certain confidence in the heart's staying power), and this list presupposes some choices: They will tell me about another candidate for a graft, apparently not in any shape, however, to survive the graft's follow-up, in particular the course of medication. I also know that I have to be grafted with a type O+ heart, thereby limiting the options. A question I will never pose: How does one decide, and who decides, when a graft, suitable for more than one graftee, is available? Here we know that the demand exceeds the supply . . . From the very outset, my survival is inscribed in a complex process interwoven with strangers and strangenesses.

Upon what does everyone's agreement on the final decision depend? Upon a survival that cannot be strictly weighed from the standpoint of pure necessity: Where would we find it? What would oblige me to live on? This opens out onto many other questions: Why me? Why live on at all? What does it mean to "live on," to "survive"? Is this even the appropriate term? In what way is a long lifespan a good thing? At this point I am fifty years old: young only for people in an "advanced" country at the end of the twentieth century . . . Only two or three centuries ago, there was nothing scandalous about dying at this age. Why can the word *scandalous* occur to me in this context today? And why, and how, for us, the "advanced" people of the year 2000, is there no longer a "right time" to die (just shy of eighty years, and it will not stop advancing)? At one point a doctor, having abandoned the quest for the cause of my cardiomyopathy, told me that "your heart was programmed to last for fifty years." But what is this program, which I cannot turn into either a destiny or a providence? Just a brief programmatic sequence in an overall lack of programming.

Where are fittingness [*justesse*] and justice here? Who measures them, who declares them? This whole thing will reach me from somewhere else and from outside—just as my heart, my body, are reaching me from somewhere else, are a somewhere else "within" me.

I do not claim to scorn quantity or to declare that nowadays we know only how to measure a lifespan and are indifferent to its "quality." I am ready to recognize that even in a formula such as "c'est toujours ça de pris" ("at least we've got that") more secrets are hidden than might be supposed. Life can only drive toward life. But it also heads toward death: Why in my case did it reach this limit of the heart? Why would it not?

Isolating death from life—without leaving one intimately entwined with the other, and each intruding into the heart of the other—this we must never do.

For eight years, during these ordeals, I will so often have heard, and will so often have repeated to myself: "But then you wouldn't be here any more!" How are we to think this kind of quasi-necessity, or desirable aspect, of a presence whose absence could always, very simply, have configured otherwise the world of various others? At the cost of some suffering? Of course. But why persist in refiguring the asymptote of an absence of suffering? An old question, but aggravated by technology, and carried by it, we have to admit, to a point where we are hardly prepared for it.

Since the time of Descartes, at least, modern humanity has transformed the longing for survival and immortality into an element in a general program of "mastery and possession of nature." It has thereby programmed the growing strangeness of "nature." It has revived the absolute strangeness of the twofold enigma of mortality and immortality. Whatever religion used to represent, humanity has carried it to a level of technical empowerment that pushes back the end in every sense of the phrase. By prolonging the term, it extends the absence of an end: prolonging what life, with what aim? To defer death is also to exhibit it, to underscore it.

We need only remark that humanity was never ready for any phase of this question and that its unreadiness for death is nothing but death itself: the blow it deals, and its injustice.

Thus, the multiple stranger intruding into my life (my thin and winded life, sometimes slipping into malaise on the edge of abandonment, simply stunned) is nothing other than death, or rather life/death: a suspension of the continuum of being, a scansion in which "I" has/have nothing much to do. Protest and acceptance alike are foreign to the situation. But nothing would not be foreign; everything is strange. In the first place, the means of survival are themselves completely strange: What does it mean to replace a heart? Representing the thing is beyond me. (Opening up the entire thorax, taking care of the graft-organ, circulating the blood outside the body, suturing the vessels . . . I know very well that surgeons insist on the insignificance of this last point: The vessels in transplants are smaller. But still: Transplanting imposes an image of passing through nothingness, a flight into space emptied of any propriety or intimacy, or else, conversely, an image of that space intruding upon the inside of me: feeds, clamps, sutures, and tubes.)

What, "properly," is this life whose "saving" is at stake? At least it's agreed, anyway, that this propriety does not reside anywhere within "my" body. It is not sited anywhere, not even in this organ whose symbolic reputation requires no further development.

(Someone will say: There is always the brain. And the idea of a brain transplant certainly makes it into the papers now and then. Some day, no doubt, humanity will raise it again. Meanwhile, we acknowledge that the brain does not survive without a remnant of the body. Conversely, and dropping the subject for now, it might survive with a whole system of foreign body grafts . . .)

A "proper" life, not to be found in any organ, and nothing without them. A life that not only lives on but continues to live properly, under a strange, threefold rule: that of decision, that of an organ, and that of sequelae to the transplant.

First of all, the graft is presented as a *restitutio ad integrum*: The heart is found to be beating once again. Here, the whole dubious symbolism of the gift of the other—a secret, ghostly complicity or intimacy between the other and me—wears out very quickly. In any event, its use, still widespread when I was grafted, seems to be disappearing bit by bit from the minds of the graftees: There's already a history of representing grafts. With the aim of stimulating organ donation, a great emphasis has been placed on the solidarity, and even the fraternity, of "donors" and recipients. And no one can doubt that this gift is now a basic obligation of humanity (in both senses of the word), or that—freed from any limits other than blood-group incompatibility (and freed especially from any ethnic or sexual limits: My heart can be a Black woman's heart)—that this gift institutes the possibility of a network where life/death is shared by everyone, where life is connected with death, where the incommunicable is in communication.

Sometimes, however, the other very quickly appears as stranger: not as a woman, a Black person, or a young man, or a Basque, but as the immunitary other, the insubstitutable other that has nonetheless been replaced. "Rejection" is its name: My immune system rejects the other's. (Which means: "I have" two systems, two immunitary identities . . .) Many suppose that rejection consists in literally spitting the heart out, vomiting it up: Indeed, the word seems to be chosen to make this plausible. That's not it, but there is certainly something unbearable about the intruder's intrusion, and it is quickly fatal if left untreated.

The possibility of rejection resides in a double strangeness: the strangeness, on the one hand, of this grafted heart, which the organism identifies and attacks as being a stranger, and, on the other hand, the strangeness of the state in which medication renders the graftee in order to protect him. It lowers the graftee's immunity, so that he can tolerate the stranger. It thereby makes him a stranger to himself, to this immunitary identity, which is akin to his physiological signature.

An intruder is in me, and I am becoming a stranger to myself. If the rejection is very strong, I need treatments to help me resist human defenses. (This is done by means of an immunoglobulin drawn from a rabbit and then assigned, as its official description specifies, to this "antihuman" use, whose surprising effects—almost convulsive tremblings—I remember very well.)

But becoming a stranger to myself does not draw me closer to the intruder. Rather, it would appear that a general law of intrusion is revealed: There has never been just one intrusion; as soon as one is produced, it multiplies itself, is identified in its renewed internal differences.

Thus, on several occasions I will know the shingles virus, or cytomegalovirus—strangers that have been dormant within me from the very start and are suddenly raised against me by the necessary immuno-depression.

At the very least, what happens is the following: Identity is equal to immunity; the one is identified with the other. To lower the one is to lower the other. Strangeness and being a stranger become common, everyday things. This gets translated through a constant exteriorization of myself: I have to be measured, checked, tested. We are flooded with warnings about the outside world (crowds, stores, swimming pools, little children, sick people). But our liveliest enemies are within: old viruses crouching all along in the shadows of immunity, having always been there, intruders for all time.

In this last instance, no possible prevention. Instead, treatments that deport to further strangenesses. They fatigue, they ruin the stomach, or there's the howling pain of shingles . . . Through it all, what "me" is pursuing what trajectory?

What a strange me!

Not because they opened me up, gaping, to change the heart. But because this gaping cannot be sealed back up. (In fact, as every X-ray shows, the sternum is stitched with filaments of twisted steel.) I am closed open. Through the opening passes a ceaseless flux of strangeness: immune-depressor medications, other medications meant to combat certain so-called secondary effects, effects that we do not know how to combat (the degrading of the kidneys), renewed controls, all existence set on a new register, stirred up and around. Life scanned and reported onto multiple registers, all of them recording other possibilities of death.

Thus, then, in all these accumulated and opposing ways, it is me that becomes my intruder.

I certainly feel it, and it's much stronger than a sensation: Never has the strangeness of my own identity, which for me has always been nonetheless so vivid, touched me with such acuity. "I" clearly became the formal index of an unverifiable and impalpable change. Between me and me, there had always been some space-time, but now there is an incision's opening and the irreconcilability of a compromised immune system.

Cancer also arrives: a lymphoma, notice of whose eventuality (certainly not a necessity; few graftees end up with it), though signaled by the cyclosporin's printed advisory, had escaped me. It comes from the lowering of immunity. The cancer is like the ragged, crooked, and devastating figure of the intruder. Strange to myself, with myself estranging me. How to say this? (But the exogenous or endogenous nature of cancerous phenomena is still being debated.)

Here too, in another way, the treatment calls for a violent intrusion. It incorporates certain amounts of chemotherapeutic and radiotherapeutic strangeness. Just as the lymphoma is eating away at the body and exhausting it, the treatments attack it, making it suffer in several ways—and this suffering links the intrusion to its rejection. Even morphine, easing pain, provokes another suffering—brutalization and spaciness.

The most elaborate treatment is called an "autograft" (or "stem-cell graft"): After relaunching my lymphocytic production through "growth factors," they take white blood cell samples for five days in a row (all the blood is circulated outside the body, the samples being taken as it flows). These they freeze. Then I am installed in a sterile chamber for three weeks, and they administer a very strong chemotherapy, leveling my marrow production before relaunching it as they reinject me with the frozen stem-cells (a strange odor of garlic pervades this injection . . .). The immune system is extremely weakened, whence the strong fevers, mycoses, and serial disorders that arise until the moment the lymphocytes start being produced again.

You come out of the whole thing bewildered. You no longer recognize yourself, but "recognize" no longer means anything. Very soon, you are just a wavering, a strangeness suspended between poorly identified states, between pains, between impotencies, between failings. Relating to the self has become a problem, a difficulty or an opacity: It happens through evil or fear, no longer anything immediate—and the mediations are tiring.

The empty identity of the "I" can no longer rely on its simple adequation (in its "I = I") as enunciated: "I suffer" implicates two I's, strangers to each other (but touching each other). The same holds for "I delight" (we could show how this is indicated by the pragmatics of either statement): In "I suffer," however, one I rejects the other, while in "I delight" one I exceeds the other. Two drops of water are doubtless no more, and no less, alike.

I end/s up being nothing more than a fine wire stretched from pain to pain and strangeness to strangeness. One attains a certain continuity through the intrusions, a permanent regime of intrusion: In addition to the more than daily doses of medicine and hospital checkups, there are the dental repercussions of the radiotherapy, along with a loss of saliva; the monitoring of food; of contagious contacts; the weakening of muscles and kidneys; the shrinking of memory and strength for work; the reading of analyses; the insidious returns of mucitis, candidiasis, or polyneuritis; and a general sense of being no longer dissociable from a network of measures and observations—of chemical, institutional, and symbolic connections that do not allow themselves to be ignored, akin to those out of which ordinary life is always woven and yet, altogether inversely, holding life expressly under the incessant warning of their presence and surveillance. I become indissociable from a polymorphous dissociation.

This has always more or less been the life of the ill and the elderly, but that's just it, I am not precisely the one or the other. What cures me is what affects or infects me; what keeps me alive is what makes me age prematurely. My heart is twenty years younger than I, and the rest of my body is (at least) twelve years older than I. Turning young and old at one and the same time, I no longer have a proper age, or properly have an age. Likewise, though not retired, I no longer properly have a trade. Likewise, I am not what I'm here to be (husband, father, grandfather, friend) without also being under the sign of this very general condition of an intruder, of various intruders who could at any moment take my place in the relation or representation to others.

In a similar movement, the most absolutely proper "I" retreats to an infinite distance (where does it go? from what vanishing point does it still proffer this as *my* body?) and plunges into an intimacy deeper than any interiority (the irreducible niche from which I say "I" but which I know to be as gaping as a chest that is opened over a void, or as a sliding into the morphine-induced unconsciousness of pain and fear mixed in abandonment). *Corpus meum* and *interior intimo meo*, the two being joined, in a complete configuration of the death of god, in order to say very precisely that the subject's truth is its exteriority and its excessiveness: its infinite exposition. The intruder exposes me to excess. It extrudes me, exports me, expropriates me. I am the illness and the medicine, I am the cancerous cell and the grafted organ, I am these immuno-depressive agents and their palliatives, I am these ends of steel wire that brace my sternum and this injection site permanently sewn under my clavicle, altogether as if, already and besides, I were these screws in my thigh and this plate inside my groin. I am turning into something like a science-fiction android, or else, as my youngest son said to me one day, one of the living dead.

We are, along with the rest of my more and more numerous fellow-creatures,³ the beginnings, in effect, of a mutation: Man begins again by passing infinitely beyond man. (This is what "the death of god" has always meant, in every possible way.) Man becomes what he is: the most terrifying and the most troubling technician, as Sophocles called him twenty-five centuries ago, who denatures and remakes nature, who recreates creation, who brings it out of nothing and, perhaps, leads it back to nothing.⁴ One capable of origin and end.

The intruder is none other than me and man himself. None other than the same, never done with being altered, at once sharpened and exhausted, denuded and overequipped, an intruder in the world as well as in himself, a disturbing thrust of the strange, the *conatus* of an on-growing infinity.

—*Translated by Richard Rand*

Postscript I (April 2005)

It has been five years since the first publication of this text. During that time, I passed the ten-year mark since the graft, which from the beginning appeared to me as a limit, the most distant horizon, which perhaps (or so I used to think) I would not even reach.

Now past this threshold, I remain wary (but quite vaguely, to tell the truth) of those hopes for life to which graftees are prone, or else I complacently believe that there are no limits, and I regain the conviction of immortality that we all share, but a conviction augmented by the assurance of already having made it past the critical term at least twice.

There are moments when I grow fearful of all the damage that so many years of chemo have done and of the strain this has placed on a heart functioning under such delicate conditions, and then there are moments when the amount of time now behind me seems, on the contrary, to be the surest sign of stability and of a long continuation.

In one way or another, a new strangeness has taken hold of me. I don't know very clearly anymore on what grounds I am surviving or whether I really have the means or even the right to do so. (Surviving, living on—Derrida had made this into a concept in his own way. It has already been six months since he left us. There are no grafts for the pancreas.) Of course, this feeling comes to the surface only rarely and fleetingly. Mostly I don't think about it, just as I spend less time at the hospital (which for this reason is losing the familiarity it had taken on). But when this thought occurs to me, I understand also that I no longer have an intruder inside me: I have become the intruder; it is as an intruder that I spend my time in a world in which my presence may well be too artificial, or even illegitimate.

Is this heightened consciousness not simply also a banal awareness of my very simple and ordinary contingency? Is it not this simplicity to which I am led back and exposed again by technical ingenuity? This thought gives me a very singular joy.

Postscript II (January 2010)
For Joanna

    The new edition of a book does not usually lead me to make any additions or transformations. I prefer in general that a book remain within the bounds of its initial form. If something else needs to be said, this can serve as the opening of a new text, not a prolongation or an addition to the first.

    With this book things are different. The new editions seem to arrive at opportune moments in order to punctuate the uninterrupted movement in which this heart continues to beat. Five years ago, I thus noted the thought of "living on" that came to me from having made it ten years since the graft. Today I am not far from twenty years—which, if I make it that far, will be in 2011. This survival appears more and more to me as a supplementary or even excedentary life. Yet more life granted to this living being, which a mechanical and chemical intrusion drew away from the death that it had coming to it, a death of its own.

In the meantime, others disappear around me. I noted this for Derrida in 2005; I must do so this time for Lacoue-Labarthe: For him too no graft was able to repair his body, for which he himself had been a fierce and stubborn intruder, poisoning it with tobacco and alcohol—and with this very bitter toxin that seeps from the feeling of not being or doing what one should.

At least I am allowed to think that if the survival machine seizes up, I can only blame it on the normal wear of machines. I do not have to undergo the fatal blow of a cancer or the gnawing of my life by my thought.

The wear of the machine leads to new intrusions. My left hip was repaired with screws after an accident that had happened long before, and with time a prosthesis had recently become necessary. But after the introduction of the titanium pin into the bone, my heart—which I always call "my own" without any second thoughts—had a "pause" (this was their word). They observed, they concluded that there was a permanent disturbance. Hence the introduction of a pacemaker—I like this word in English, I regret not having a French version: *faiseur de pas* (maker of steps, paces), *cadenceur* (cadence inducer) . . . ? But the probe thus introduced into the heart provoked the formation of a colony of *candida* (a "yeast" or "fungus"). A virulent endocarditis set in; the pacemaker had to be removed immediately. During the treatment for the infection, the heart was treated with a product administered intravenously. Then they added another contraption, this one "epicardiac," meaning that no part of it penetrates the heart. It was placed in my abdomen, where it formed a small bump that had never been there, discreet but sometimes palpable. An intruder pressed up against the first intruder—and in the abdomen, a milieu completely different from the ribcage: not a structure but a zone, a region of passages, exchanges, osmoses, not of pulsations and flows. As if the mechanical (itself electronic) were making a real intrusion into the organic. In fact, as I understand it more and more, there are several organisms, including at the very least the mechanical, the chemical, the nervous, the sensorial, and the visceral. The intruder gives me a looser and less rigid perception of this assemblage that comes together as "me."

Is there some relation with the episode that followed a few months later? A pulmonary embolism (edema, shortness of breath), which did not help with the poor state of the tricuspid valve (another sharp and powerful name). They didn't know. In any case, they still had to thin the blood while continuing the antifungal treatment. The pharmacological intrusion turned into impregnation and infusion.

At the same time, the H_1N_1 virus follows the course of its epidemic, which may or may not be a pandemic. But graftees must be vaccinated—with two injections, even. Likewise at the same time, debates rage about the steps that must be taken, or not, to prevent the very serious environmental degradations whose signs are more credible than ever. And I think: When there are shortages of water and air, of food, of energy, what will happen with grafts? They are a remarkable example of how technical processes lead to—and link together with—yet more technical processes, in an indefinite chain, just as medical knowledge and procedures are constantly refined, become less rigid and more flexible, even as they oblige us to tighten all the links between the techniques they mobilize.

It remains the case, for the moment, that in fact the idea of intrusion continues to fade: Everything is intrusive in this inextricable interlacing of "nature" and "artifice" that forms the human world, that is to say the world, absolutely and with no outside. In truth, this intrication gives me less and less the feeling of being a stranger or a foreigner—to what "natural" order would I be foreign?—and more and more the awareness of an ever-growing familiarity with this fixed-up, cobbled-together, mix-and-match body.[5] Because this body is so, because it triggers all these episodes, interventions, and transformations, it is close to me in an intimacy of which I would no doubt be completely unaware if I were simply my age. To be sure, I am the age of my graft. But I am also *hors d'âge*, as one says of a bottle of very fine spirits.

Am I a kind of drunkenness to myself? No doubt. At times it is light and floating, and at times vertiginous and heavy, but it is never something that leaves me in the simple certainty of being "myself." To feel that such a thing as "self" is infinitely far behind or before me—that is the sensation, the sentiment, the sense that no signification and no identity would be able to saturate.

Postscript III (August 2017)

(1) In 2014 I was asked to write a few words on the occasion of the publication of a novel whose subject was a heart transplant. I wrote the following note, under the title "A Long-Term Heart [*Un coeur au long cours*]":

Twenty-two years ago—almost twenty-three—my heart was grafted into me. From what I understand, it has now just about overtaken the age of my donor ("my" donor? a strange way to talk . . . yes, he or she gave me back to myself). Between him or her and me there are none of the things that people often like to evoke: secret communications, spiritual osmoses, intermingled identities. All this is good for fantasies, whether for graftees themselves occasionally, or much more often for those in search of strong sensations. But a life lived as a gift received goes far beyond these supposed frissons. It is a life that depends on the sharing not only of another life but of life itself, first of all in its capacity to make an organ function outside the organism in which it was formed and after the death of this organism. But this life would hardly be able to last if the living-speaking being, the one that knows how to extend and refashion nature, had not invented the means for transmitting it. Around five hundred thousand years ago, this being found a way to transmit fire. And later, warnings and messages. Then provisions, ornaments, thoughts. Ways of being and appearing, forms of culture. Finally, today, it transmits life, not through generation but by shielding from death a palpitation that, passing from one to another, pursues an elementary rhythm. Today we have recently created an electric heart able to beat out this rhythm: I imagine the absence of immunological problems that this would make possible, but also the other difficulties that will have to be discovered and surmounted. For all those like me who live from another human heart, the decisive problem is that of maintaining an immunitary balance. This maintenance eventually turns the body into "a real chemical factory," as one doctor said to me. One must constantly manage this factory (while also living as much as possible without thinking about it).

The graftee exists in a technical mode, that is, according to ends that were not given in advance (neither nature, nor providence, nor destiny). Ends that exceed finality or purposiveness: Is it the graft that lives for me, or I for it? And in the end, what is the end, the purpose, of existence? The graft is a philosopher disguised as a devil. Here, in "me," the life that is expressed as living beings and as living-thinking, living-calculating, living-imagining beings—this life has invented for itself another life and a life that is other. We are experimental laboratories, lands of immigration, bearers and poets of a new fire.

Fire warms, but it also burns. I think of the extreme case of a woman who was grafted with a liver while in a hepatic coma.

She was ill at ease with this intrusion and, looking for some words from a graftee, she found my book The Intruder. *We became friends. She stopped thinking of herself as having been violently assaulted by technology. And yet technology certainly is violent; it ravages the earth, the sea, and the sky from which it was born. It has deployed the system of appropriation called "capitalism" while never ceasing to displace and transform every supposed "natural property." We must recognize that our experience is ambiguous: Either we find ourselves transplanted into another life, or else we are grafted onto the monstrous body of a techno-capitalist Leviathan. "Democracy" too is an experiment that oscillates between these two outer edges. Either/or: Kierkegaard spoke of this alternative, which gives its contours to the necessity of decision—of this decision that can only take place in the undecidable, as Derrida said (for whom it was not possible to graft a pancreas). Which means that we have to decide: Either we let a blind process appropriate our existences, or we reappropriate the process ourselves.*

The life of a graftee can be seen as a microcosm of the general mutation of the world and of humanity. Exuberance of life or expropriation of the living: What is certain is that we can decide only if we know how to think the "proper." Is it an originary possession? an inalienable singularity? or does "the free use of the proper" of which Hölderlin spoke amount to making use of everything without being enslaved to anything, not even an imaginary "oneself"? or ought this free use make us understand that every "self" is made up of encounters and occurrences, of pieces and fragments, of additions and withdrawals? Yes, and it's in this sense that "I is an other"—or "others," as another poet put it (Deguy). Neither the body nor the soul that is its form is perfectly fitted to an essence, but each occasion of existing offers the chance and the risk of inventing, of grafting, of modulating a new rhythm, a new way of being.

(2) In 2016 I celebrated the twenty-fifth anniversary of the graft with the Eastern Association of Graftees. A few months later, two hundred of us heart graftees, along with our doctors and nurses, celebrated thirty years since heart transplantation had begun to be practiced in the city of Strasbourg.

Of course, there is no real local specificity to such a practice, but there is, as with all things, a personality, a climate that is born from the simple fact of proximity and continuity. For me, this is a bit like Strasbourg in general, a place onto which I found myself grafted more than fifty years ago. One is always more or less grafted onto places, groups, networks, people. Or they are grafted onto us. If I write "our" doctors, "our" nurses, this is not possessive, but rather—how can I say this?—attached . . .

This means that we swarm, we teem with intruders and intrusions. (Note that I am writing this in August 2017, as refugees and migrants from Syria, Sudan, and elsewhere continue to be pressed all the way to Europe and beyond— and to be pushed by counterpressures back over borders and even into the sea—while between the countries of Europe there are continual tensions around the circulation, exchange, and evaluation of the commodity known as "labor power" or "capacity." Whereas "labor" itself is constantly displaced, delocalized, revalued, transplanted, and grafted onto forms ever more distant from those we have so long associated with human labor.)

More and more the technics of grafting—whose agricultural form dates from time immemorial—appears as a sort of metatechnics: the art of combinations, supplementations, prostheses, regenerations, inscriptions, transferrals, transpositions, transactions . . . We don't know where to stop the series of linkages, and perhaps, rather, the contagion or contamination, not to say the transfusion, if not the confusion, of so many operations now so characteristic of the general combinatory in which we are caught up and carried away.

Jacques Derrida had sensed this, had a presentiment of it, and thought it through better than anyone. It was he who most clearly discerned that what is at stake here is the proper, properness, property, propriety—in all the senses and connotations of these terms. Much more profoundly than the possession of an object, it is the appropriation of a subject to itself that is in question. The grafting of a heart is but a still distant image—or manifestation—of what in every "being a self" (of a person, of a country, of a language, of a thought) implies a host of intrusions. Without these intrusions nothing would take place, nothing would begin to individuate or identify itself.

Nothing seems to me more important—I would even say more imperious—for thought today than to advance in what no doubt remains obscure and resists any central disposition of our Western culture, but that precisely insists with such force only to the extent that this civilization, having been spread and grafted everywhere, no longer recognizes itself and enters into a radical mutation (that is, an uprooting, for this is what a true "radicality" implies).

(3) *How are you holding up?* ask those who are intrigued by twenty-six years of the graft. The question is not idle. Natural aging is modified both for better and for worse. Without the intruder, I would have lived twenty-six fewer years—and it's not completely finished. But with it, and with the biochemistry everywhere grafted onto my biology, there is no lack of complications.

Now this is exactly the issue: A biology that is somehow one's own or "proper" to oneself, a biological or physiological idiosyncrasy, never exists without encountering the same complexities, obscurities, and strangenesses as a psychic, affective, intellectual, and moral "personality." The graft is precisely a good occasion for grasping—the better to ungrasp and release it—the perfectly evanescent and elusive unity of an ego or a "me." Perfectly identical to itself, no doubt, but identical only insofar as it eludes itself at every moment.

Just now during a trip to Tokyo I had to be hospitalized because of some health problems. These problems are not connected to the graft, but it is always necessary to take it into account. There was much talk, some ten years ago, about the difficulties that grafting would encounter in Japan because of the religious nonrecognition of brain death. It is interesting that grafts that involve dead "donors" are sometimes frowned upon for various religious reasons or for reasons of representation (mutilation of the body): Grafting cannot be separated from a cultural milieu any more than from a technical context. But what culture is truly able to grapple with all that technics makes possible? Certainly not a simple culture of "progress" measured solely by the prolongation of life. A prolonged life does not necessarily have more "sense" than a shortened one. Is there a correct, just, or proper duration of a human life?

The idea of grafting is much more accepted in Japan today. But this does not mean that certain forms of religious adherence have been entirely abandoned there or that these are disappearing to the same extent as our religious practices have. That said, an artificial heart will soon perhaps render grafting itself archaic.

However that may be, technical globalization has so far not eliminated differences in social custom. Same medicine, another world. Same molecules but given in different doses, insofar as there may be differences in physiology between Asians and Europeans. Same operational protocols but different relations—or I would say: different music, since I don't understand the meaning, the sense of the words spoken. A gentler music . . .

My stay in Japan has been completely upended: On the one hand, it's been ruined, but on the other, it is transfigured by the warmth of the Japanese friends who have stayed near me. This postscript is dedicated to them.

—Translated by Jeff Fort

Toward Nancy

Jean-Luc Nancy: But it's a bit odd, after all, what you're saying: You wanted to be as imperceptible as possible, when you arrived in France, because imperceptible, taken literally, means that no one sees you. When what you wanted was not to be seen as a foreigner.

Ana Samardzija: I wanted to gain entry, to be there. Not to be seen as different, above all not to disturb the order of things. Not to lay myself open to being rejected or expelled.

How did this idea come to you, the idea of an intrusion that is necessarily borne by the foreigner, the stranger?

JLN: It came to me because of what we were talking about a moment ago, this question of a double bind related to the foreigner, because when one day I was asked to write something on foreignness, on strangeness, on the fact of being a stranger, a foreigner, my first reaction was to get away from the conventional idea of welcoming the foreigner. We all agree on the necessity of welcoming the foreigner. We can even say that this is what we *want*, but there is precisely a certain way of insisting on, of emphasizing—of normalizing, too, of making it a norm—the welcoming of the foreigner, the welcoming of differences, the respect for the other, etc. A way that, in the end, amounts to acting as if there were no strangeness or foreignness at all. It's as if one wanted to pretend that a Black man is not Black. And so I said to myself at that moment that what I would like to do is to try to say what in the foreigner should remain foreign, what should remain strange, otherwise he is not a foreigner, not a stranger.

AS: When you wrote: *There must be something of an intruder in the foreigner,* to whom is this addressed? To the one who welcomes the foreigner, or to the foreigner?

JLN: First, of course, I was thinking, as you say, of the one who welcomes. This is a way to ask: What does it mean *to welcome*? If we insist that a welcome must lead to assimilation, well . . . this is one of the words that have been used for the relation with foreigners, with immigrants. And often people have also spoken of the American concept of the "melting pot." I'm not sure how one now distinguishes between integration and assimilation. But what I do know is that all the discourses on welcoming differences that aim at a sort of erasure of differences are like what you were saying about making yourself imperceptible. This means that when I "don't see you," I don't see differences. This comes up against the fact that differences exist. There are strong poles of assimilation or of integration. So what I'm saying is that it's a question of how to think beyond these models, which no longer work.

[*Pause*]

I have the feeling, and this is something that is said sometimes, that France is a country that can particularly make one feel like an intruder. Because a country with a strong identity, with an arrogant behavior or mentality, as we often hear . . .

AS: I'm not at all sure about that. Do you have this impression? Because, at the same time . . .

JLN: [*slight laughter*] Do I have the impression of being arrogant? Well, yes, seriously, in a certain way. When the French lecture the rest of the world about assimilation, integration, they say this from the high horse of an identity, a strong identity, undeniably strong, perhaps less strong than a century ago, but it is strong, and it was built through centuries of domination, through a very centralized and very strong state that pushed toward the integration of an entire set of French provinces, of languages, of cultures, etc. Through wars.

AS: Doesn't it seem to you that what is called Schengen Europe, that is, a Europe that is finally very closed to the outside, gives rise precisely—how to say this?— to clandestine or intrusive passage into the interior? Because it's difficult to gain entry except through intrusion.

JLN: Of course. In fact I believe that intrusion is produced precisely by homogenization and by a strong immunization. And I think that this is something that exists in not only Schengen Europe but in every civilization that is a civilization of homogenization, that has tended to homogenize the world. One does speak . . . always, in a way, either in terms of an unfortunate homogenization or in terms of a joyous heterogeneity . . . and the one against the other. And the intrusion is really . . . look at the people in [the refugee camp at] Sangatte. These are people who are excluded from Schengen Europe, some because they are Europeans from outside the Schengen Area and others because they come from very distant parts of the world. These are people who are asking to enter a homogeneous space. And who hope at the same time to be able in this space to hold on to what one calls an identity, but an identity that ought to be able to avoid the assumption that it is intrusive . . . but that ought to be able to be heterogeneous within the homogeneous, nonetheless.

AS: Which means that something arrives, something happens to homogeneity insofar as the intruder gains entry, enters in. What happens to . . .

JLN: When there is an intrusion, there is some disorder, there is something of a jolt, a shock, and something of a threat. An intruder is always threatening. Well, I don't know . . . the word *intruder* always refers immediately to a kind of threat. And you know, I have noticed that the word *intrusion* is often used by psychoanalysts to speak of phenomena that arise in consciousness or in someone's mind in a way that is violent, threatening, even hallucinatory, and these are called *intrusions*.

AS: This is an intrusion of the other in the self.

JLN: But at the same time, what manifests itself there in a pathological way is also the same thing that can be a strangeness to myself, a foreignness within me, something in this "me" that I could not even call *an other* but the fact that there is something other, something of the other, and this is not at all pathological. It's something that cannot be identified. So if thinking is always a process of identifying, then this is something one cannot think.

AS: And so . . .

JLN: This is the limit . . . this is precisely the limit of identity, but there is no identity except also through something of this intrusion. Because an identity that is full, that is solid and uniform, and that precisely can no longer allow for any intrusion . . . such an identity is also stupid, closed, and sealed off . . .

AS: It's the identity of a stone.

JLN: Yes, a stone, yes . . .

AS: There must be something of the other, but at the same time there must also be a kind of rejection of the other, no?

JLN: Yes, just as there must be acceptance and rejection and not acceptance of rejection . . . and just as [one can say that] these voices . . . that when someone hears voices, this can be madness, or genius. I don't know, but you see, without wanting to play into the romanticism of genius, there is something true, something that has tried to express itself, in saying that it is always another voice that speaks through our voice, when we truly say something.

AS: When you say: There must be something of the intruder in the foreigner . . . when I hear this, I hear it as a call. Something that says: "Come, but come as a foreigner, a stranger, but come when I don't expect it, and . . . surprise me!"

JLN: That's true, except it's an impossible call, because if I say to you "surprise me," you can surprise me only by not responding directly to this demand I am making.

AS: This means that for there to be something surprising, I must not be waiting, expecting to be surprised.

JLN: That's it, but then at the moment when one is not expecting . . . then one no longer accepts either.

AS: So one is irritated, disturbed . . .

JLN: Yes, that's it. And one cannot escape from this difficulty.

AS: One is disturbed, but at the same time something arrives, something happens that allows us to become other.

JLN: Yes. But precisely, that is really something that one cannot want or will. It's somewhat, I think it's somewhat like in life, for me, I am always very struck by the fact that . . . *everything* of importance that has happened to me . . . I mean, everything that has determined important things in my life, of course it has come without my foreseeing it. I have never foreseen anything . . . not even my profession . . . No, it's true! It has always come from elsewhere.

[*The glass door to the train compartment slides open. A man enters and takes a seat, interrupting the conversation. A few seconds pass before he speaks.*]

Alex Descas: You know how long until we arrive?

JLN: Pardon?

AD: Do you know how long it will be until we arrive?

JLN: Ah, how long it will be. We arrive in ten minutes.

AD: Already. It's been quick and enjoyable.

JLN: Yeah . . . a bit long though, wasn't it?

—Translated by Jeff Fort

The Intruder According to Claire Denis

I

It would be fair to expect the author of the book *The Intruder* to speak to the effect made on him by the film that claims to have found "an inspiration" in that book. But that is not what I am going to do. Or, rather, I will do so only as part of an attempt to untangle something of what this film has, in turn, inspired in me. Moreover, I will not be analyzing whatever relationship Claire Denis may have established with my book. That relationship, that reading, must remain her secret and hers alone—even as the film constitutes its irreducible transmission.

Let us clarify right away for those who don't already know: The book contains no story that the film could have adapted (except by transforming itself into a medical documentary, which would not really have preserved any "inspiration" from the book). As I once put it—struck by the assonance between words—Claire Denis did not adapt my book; she adopted it. (And in fact, her film does address adoption.) The relationship between us is not the relatively "natural" one presumed of an adaptation (a simple change of register or instrument) but the kind of extranatural relationship that, without evidence of kinship, depends solely on its symbolic elaboration. That this, in the final analysis, is the truth behind all kinship is perhaps one of the lessons of the film, just as my book suggests that in the end there is no "real body"—and this "just as" is already enough to engage the complex and delicate system of correspondences, of "inspirations," or contagions between us.

The book merely records a brief reflection on what a heart transplant might represent in the context of a contemporary understanding of identity. The "intruder" here designates an irreducible, and yet incorporated, alterity for which the transplant itself is only a figure—the central piece of a more general process of transformation that affects everything we believe to be "natural," entering the realm of what I have elsewhere termed our *écotechnie*. A far cry from the complex, if not labyrinthine, plot of a film in which a persecuted man with a damaged heart seeks a transplant so that he can pursue his search for an abandoned son.

A far cry, and yet . . . It's enough to juxtapose the arguments, thus condensed, of the book and the film to reveal a glimmer: If filiation can be considered an image (metaphor and metonymy at once) of naturalness [*la naturalité*] in general, then the film undeniably questions, complicates, and suspends the very idea or hypothesis of this naturalness. One might even ask if naturalness isn't its primary subject. The breadth and beauty of the landscapes of two hemispheres lend their images a force apart from any aestheticized settings: The question arises—for example, in a long static shot of dawn rising over the violet sea of the islands—concerning the nature of nature (if you will) for us today and of the possibility or impossibility of continuing to inhabit the earth. (An attempt at inhabitation, at returning home, comprises the penultimate movement of the film, no less ambiguously than the others.)

I suspect that what I have encountered here is—at least from one angle, one approach—the invisible source of the "inspiration" of this film and that I will thus be able to understand how, in spite of the indisputable, irreducible, and welcome heterogeneity that separates the film from the book, the former doubles back on the latter, pulling it into its ebb tide, beyond itself.

Let us follow the thread that has already been identified, that of a "denaturation." We will see that this thread is woven from several strands. I'll just mention those I have identified, which fall into three pairings: "father and son," "Christ and Dionysus," "woman and dogs." In each of these registers, perhaps (for I am only making gestures here, sketches really), a form of intrusion will occur that will unravel or frustrate the "naturalness" that we might expect (that of "father," of "god," of "woman"). These correspond also to the strands braided by the film in its editing, full of ellipses, its images with broad, flat fields of color, or in its quickly passing mobile shots and rapid breakaways. It is the rhythm of a startled, syncopated thinking—a thinking occupied less with its "ideas" than with its movement, with its pace and its displacement. As is said in the film by the merchant selling an expensive watch with a transparent casing: You can appreciate the beauty of the movement. This watch, completely extraneous to the plot, is the film itself; just as the dogsled driver in the final shots, laughing while she tears through the icy forest on a race without a destination, is also the film. As is the woman who is shooting the film and who runs along with it; the woman who runs in the film until she is outside it, until she draws it out of itself, with a pleasure that is redoubled when it jumps off the screen.

II

At one level, the idea of simple, biological filiation is conspicuously staged close to the film's beginning, in which Trébor's son is shown in his function of father (of two very young children), of domestic man (he paints a ceiling), and of progenitor (he makes love to his young wife, whose breasts in turn serve as a reminder, by way of a droll juxtaposition with baby bottles, of the parent-infant relationship). One could argue that the father is purposely shown playing a *role*, beginning with the shot in which he is cropped between the frames of two windows. Now this son, we will learn, is decidedly not the "beloved son": That role belongs rather to the son whom Trébor abandoned in Tahiti, where he will later go to look for him. For this other son, Trébor will have a boat made, because "my son is a good sailor": *a good sailor,* without a doubt what Trébor himself had been or wanted to be in his youth, when he set off for the Marquesas Islands, as we will see in a flashback (which incorporates an old, unfinished film by Paul Gégauff with a rather ominous title—*Le reflux, The Ebb Tide*—starring a young Michel Subor).

The basic premise, then, involves a disturbance that affects filiation—or rather, is effected on filiation—by way of an inexplicable, unmotivated preference, a choice between two sons and a preference for the one who represents youth (idealized, of course) but who is also abandoned, presumably because his mother was a foreigner from the distant South Pacific, a Marquesan woman loved and left behind during his travels. It's also why the theme of family is introduced only after another theme that opens the film, that of crossing borders and the illegal transport of goods—by way of the young mother, in her role as a customs canine enforcement officer who inspects suspicious cargo. Right away, via this young couple and the double theme they embody, an order is established, of legitimate lineage and authorized passage, which might justifiably be called a natural political economy. In these terms, Trébor's heart transplant is but a restoration of integrity, a renewal of vigor that will allow him to move ahead. But the transplant, as well as the purchase of the boat, involves large sums of money, manifestly illegal and no less manifestly stolen from the first son (a double illegality of sorts: In the end, Trébor robs everyone, including, finally, himself).

We learn that the abandoned son has become the lamented son. Trébor would like to retrieve him—*le retrouver,* from *trouver* (to find). And doesn't the fact that *trouver* evokes his name—even in English, by way of *trover,* which comes from *trouvere* (therefore from *trobar,* the root of *troubadour*)—lend a poetic touch to what we might call "the invention of the son"? (In French it's used as a first name, while in English it signifies "skill," but the French also have the nautical term *tribord.*) Trébor wants to uncover—or, rather, discover for the first time—this image, this idea of successful filiation; this would be something like a return home. "I want to welcome my son home," he says as he settles into the hut that he has rediscovered. It's a meager, dilapidated shack, where a fragment of mosquito netting flutters in the breeze like a ghost. Trébor's desire is to follow the ghosts, to make manifest the true face of his son—of himself, of love, of the natural order restored. At the closing of the boat purchase, the Korean ship owner lifts his glass and says, "Let us celebrate the love between a father and his son." Trébor toasts and drinks, but the strength of the alcohol makes him hiccup. He says, "It's strong!"—as if responding, with absolute ambiguity, to the ship owner's words.

Henri, Trébor's Marquesan friend and onetime cohort, begins the search for a substitute son, arranging for a village council to interview candidates. This highly irregular casting call illuminates the subject's complexity: A social structure of the "archaic" world easily assumes the task of providing an invented son for a man who had, for a brief moment long ago, been one of their own. The scene operates both as a theatricalization of the work of the imagination or of idealization and as dramaturgy of the art and artifacts structuring kinship. None of the young people meets the requirement of physical resemblance, the only requirement possible in the absence of all other criteria; in lieu of the real son, a boy who resembles the father and whose skin tone is consistent with having mixed blood would be enough to imitate nature.

But this art of discovery fails. Resemblance, the sign and signature of nature, is not to be found [*introuvable*]. In the state of nature, Trébor can only be the big white body sunbathing naked in the forest, asleep with his dogs, at the beginning of the film or the swimmer, the cycler, the athletic body occupied only with itself. Could he even have a legitimate son? Does he himself know? The boy who ends up taking the son's place does so purely on his own initiative, by his own insistence: He opposes himself to Trébor before imposing himself on him (but by then Trébor, weakened, isn't at home anymore, has had to be hospitalized). The boy refuses money; he will not enter into the cycle of (false) common value. And he is a surfer: a wholly different species, of a different era, practicing a different kind of "seafaring."

In fact this son, who has not been adopted, who has in a sense transplanted himself into Trébor's life (he comes to the hospital, he puts on scrubs), is also the one who will locate the trace of the first son and who will make it possible for the origin of the transplanted heart—taken from this murdered first son—to be revealed.

In a way, the familial loop closes with this terrible return of the heart of the son into the chest of the father. A terrible return with implications of murder and revenge, of the complex cruelty used by Trébor's creditors to get him to pay (they tell him his debt is inextinguishable). Possibly this horror is also, in whole or in part, a product of Trébor's delusion: He could have imagined the consequences of the misdeed (the crime, to be accurate) from which he has benefited or the familial provenance of the heart (how could he not have created a fantasy, even a fleeting one, about the provenance of his transplanted heart, about his paternity?).

In the end, Trébor leaves on a boat, accompanied by the coffin of the dead son whose heart lives inside him and by Toni, who pampers him with care. We might think he is returning to the island where he had hoped to wait for his son—toward the island, toward solitude, nature, the immemorial. But really, he is returning to nothing but his own death; at least, that is the best we can deduce from his condition. Or maybe to a life hanging from a thread . . . The return will not bring him back to a point of departure, to an origin, and the Polynesian "paradise" escapes into the night—making way for a snowy finale in the Northern Hemisphere.

Genealogies are vague and distant, improbable, or at least uncertain. That's what we are told by the photographs of the Chinese ancestors of the businessmen Trébor talks to in Papeete. It's not about generations or heritage: It's about departure, passage, drift, and the law that no return can ever amount to a return to the same. The intrusion of the other is the rule. If there is a hidden political message in this film, it's one that refuses any assumption of identity or "naturalness," including—and this is its most subtle point—identities labeled "mixed" or "Creole." Intrusion is stronger, less reducible, and more troubling than any mixture, for it goes from like to like; here, from Trébor to Trébor.

III

Travel, displacement, change of place via intrusion, and escape; displacement across countries or oceans (the label "Wild Pacific" sewn on a pair of jeans); the friction between languages (we hear French, Russian, Korean, Tahitian, dogs); and the movement of time both measured (a precious watch) and without measure (we are given no temporal reference for the transplant, the convalescence, or the healing of the scar, a period of time conspicuously subtracted from the film's duration)—this mobile whole, fluid and shifting, provides the guiding schema of the film. The sliding motions of swimming or biking; the movement of cars, dog races, planes, and boats; a walker's wanderings, a surfer's glide: The movement of the film, its *kinaesthesia*, is a movement of movements and of sensations of movements, culminating in the fierce momentum of the dog sled and the driver's whip.

This isn't to say that time counts; rather, it counts in every sense: It is precious (like the watch), like the time of return and the time of the quest, like the time of memory and time of waiting, like the time of tension and the time of release. As with the watch purchased in Geneva, home to the industries of precise timekeeping and unified banking, time counts both absolutely and not at all: Every instant is precious, but all instants sink into the general equivalence of their own displacement.

In a parallel fashion, time is mechanical, adjusted, counted—like the regular pulsing of a heart, a machine defined by the fact of beating—and *at the same time* it is continuous and fluid, variable, elastic, and unpredictable. That is how we must "appreciate the beauty of the movement." Duration perseveres and pauses at the same time; it is continuously shot through with holes or outmaneuvered by ellipses, by mystifying flashbacks or uncertain simultaneities.

To look at just one example and not the least: The burial that takes place fairly early in the film, which isn't very specifically located (probably in Papeete), could be that of Trébor himself, or of his son, or could even be an anonymous burial with symbolic value. We will not know anything with certainty; all we have are the slow advance of the coffin in close-up and the words of the priest.

The mutual intrusion of time and place, along with that of persons, is in a very literal way the most central idea of the film. Almost every image is imprinted with a strong sign, a mark of intrusion similar to the scar—the bumps and craters on Trébor's skin; the beauty marks on his lover's body or on the dog trainer's breasts; the eyes of the blind masseuse, which are themselves like scars; or a clock tower in the sky in Geneva, furtive shadows in the forest, the minuscule light glimmering in the distance on the banks of the violet sea. Like Trébor's scar and the surface of the sea, all skins are marked by experience, damaged, pitted, and marred, sensitive, exposed.

Likewise, when the young couple—the son and the customs guard—encounter a group of hikers in the forest, she says, "They don't have the right shoes," and he responds, "You notice everything." It could be that they are poorly equipped hikers or perhaps phony hikers or other fugitives trying to make it through during the day. We won't find out which, and this isolated scene inscribes itself on the film like the inclusion of a doubt, an intrusion into the story as much as into the mountainous frontier.

At the midpoint of the film there is, like an explosion of the image, the leaping cascade of multicolored ribbons, marking the Korean ritual of a boat's baptism. It's like an effusion of shimmering celluloid unspooling from a paper balloon—as if from the heart of the film—in a mixture of joy, festivity, and irony.

IV

Another possible interpretive thread—which, if followed, yields almost a different film—hovers just beneath the surface of the first; it's a vision, like the bodies trapped under ice, as plausible as it is unreal, dreamlike. Who is dead? Who has been killed? Who is left over, trapped under the ice? Whose heart do the dogs seize in their jaws? There are answers to these questions, but the answers are designed to be clouded, unclear—as are death and life as well. The intrusion, then, may be that of each of these into the other.

The foreign body, in this second interpretation, could be identified as that of Christ or at least that of a Christ-like figure. This proposition may seem outlandish, and perhaps it is. However, it can't be set aside without first looking at a series of clues (whose limited number throughout the film is no reason to discount their importance). Any one of these clues is enough to establish a christic reference. It doesn't matter if Claire Denis and her cowriter are conscious of it or not; we recall that the reference was present, too, in *Beau travail* (and in that case was at the very heart of the text that inspired the film, Melville's *Billy Budd*.)

To begin with, there is the series of crosses, of which the first, at least, is very deliberately foregrounded in the frame: a wooden cross, unadorned, planted in the forest in the Jura and filmed in such a manner that it occupies nearly the whole screen, "crossing" it, as it were, and imprinting on the film a sort of double emblem—the sign of a kind of crusade and of the cross hairs of a viewfinder through which we are invited to look.

This image is not accidental, and it is hard not to see a connection to the ones that follow: a cross etched on a clock in Geneva amid falling snow, a small iron cross taking up much of the frame, and another even smaller and more discreet cross embroidered into the pattern of a curtain in Papeete. Then there is the solemn advance—during a tumultuous lightning storm, no less—of the gold crucifix adorning the coffin carried by four men into a church where a priest, touching it, delivers a homily that will be revisited later in the film. And finally, how not to see the shape of a half-cross formed by the scar of the graft?

Add to this series of crosses another set of clues, less immediately resonant but that point even more decisively to a christic interpretation, and it becomes impossible not to consider it—even if there is no question of arriving at any conclusion.

The "real" son (whether actually real or imaginary) is called the "beloved son" in a letter that Trébor leaves half-burned (as if it's meant to be found), which gets deciphered by the "real" son once he has become worried about his father's absence. "Beloved son" is, according to the common translations, how a "celestial voice" designates Jesus during his baptism in the River Jordan. Later, in Tahiti, as we begin to understand that the beloved son is possibly not of this world (to put it in evangelical terms!), we are shown the digging of a grave. We do not know for whom the grave is intended any more than we knew who is in the coffin or if the coffin will go into the grave (the constant reign of indecision between life and death, the living and the dead). The grave-digging scene ends with a deliberately strange still frame shot, like a posed photo, in which the motionless workers, leaning on their spades, frame the empty pit as if giving it center stage. The empty grave, of course, makes a symbolic gesture toward resurrection. It is clear that the entire logic of homecoming described previously can be duplicated in the logic of resurrection: not only that of Trébor, thanks to the transplant (it is banal to say that someone who has had a heart transplant has been "raised from the dead"), but also that of the "actual" son, whose heart lives again, lives on and survives, in his father, or even that of the "real" son, who is (re)incarnated by the grace of Toni.

Christ's resurrection is followed by his ascension. Here, the body of the tortured son (it is his torture that is on display at the morgue, in his badly stitched-up chest) is hoisted into the air by a forklift and put on board the boat for what will be the final voyage of Trébor and his "sons." The camera films this ascension from the ground, in a long low-angle shot that serves to glorify the body, enveloped in its waxed case. A heavy ascension, yes; a mechanical and conspicuously filmic one—but for all that, still distinguished from religious phantasmagoria by way of a true elevation of the gaze.

The link between the cross and ascension is clear, and there is no need to comment further on it. I have no desire to string together a Christology that has no place here. I will only point out that according to a certain, fairly common, tradition—let us say from the epistles of James to Nietzsche—Christ is portrayed as an intruder, a disturbing presence bringing trouble and a fear of foreignness to the world.

Of course, explicit scriptural reference is not wholly absent from the film. What we hear from the priest during the burial is a passage from Revelation that contains three salient points: On the one hand, God says that he is "the Alpha and the Omega" and that he is the one who dispenses from "the spring of the water of life"; on the other hand, he proclaims an heir who "will be His son" in this life; finally, he places in opposition to this son of "renewed" life (within the context of the passage) all the "dogs, and sorcerers, and whoremongers, and murderers, and idolaters, and whosoever loveth and maketh a lie" who are headed toward the "second death"—that is, who will not be resurrected. Thus, the themes of life and the son are joined by the less explicit theme of possible damnation for Trébor (who has certainly murdered) and, perhaps, for everyone else . . .

For all this, the point is not simply to identify religious references in the film per se. What is really at play here is a relationship of intrusion—of life into death, death into life (Claire Denis called another of her films *No Fear, No Die*). This intrusion exactly doubles an unexpected intrusion into the Christ-like figure by that other mythic figure of life and death, Dionysus (whose name is echoed in "Denis"). Once he has read the letter to the "beloved son" in the cabin in the forest, that other home where the father does not await him, the "actual" son finds and picks up a crown made of leaves and flowers. It was braided and worn by the wild girl who haunts the woods, who has no relation to the protagonists except by contiguity and analogy, tied like Trébor to nature, to the sun and the lustrous water, to dogs; also like the son and the Russian thugs killed in the forest, she does not utter a single word in any of her appearances. It is quite Nietzschean, in fact: a Christ-Dionysus who, in the end, delivers the secret of life beyond all nature.

It's underscored by the editing: The Dionysian crown is braided and donned by the wild girl at the same moment when, in the cabin, Trébor and his lover are embracing.

V

We should return here once again to the idea of passage. All the movement of the film, all its *kinetics* in the strict sense, is about passage. The intruder is as much the one who passes as the one who suddenly enters. His entry is attended by his departure; they are indiscernible from each other: That is how he remains a foreigner during his passage, why he can't be identified or assigned a home. He passes, he breaches borders or fords; as when Trébor moves into the hut, the two men transport a mattress—synonym of rest and comfort—by carrying it on their heads, as if holding it high above water and danger (and now we are approaching the past, evoked by images from an old film showing these two young men caught in a storm).

This passage does not move from a present to a future. It is not a proper quest, a progress or progression, a flight, and it is not really a story. It passes from a present to its own past and does not come back to the present except to watch it pass again. Trébor's obscure Russian past pursues him; meanwhile he is trying to make amends with a lost son who doesn't want to see him again, who will lead him, in any case, nowhere but back to his own youth, the better to deliver him to his imminent and final decline, unless everything gets suspended in the immobile time of an endless passage on a boat we will never see dock, carrying the father and the two sons, one dead and the other fake, having embarked without a destination. It's a strange trinity of the heart: One man has lost his; another is running on "empty" (as the Russian woman has said to Trébor earlier); the third takes care of the others as if only he, a stranger, understands everything that the rest of us don't understand.

In an analogous manner, the film passes from one hemisphere into another, from the West to the East first and then from the North to the South—only to return *in extremis* to winter in the Jura. There has been no progress, no more than Polynesia could be taken for some paradise. To be sure, this Polynesia is enchanted not only in Trébor's fantasy; it also saturates the images of luxurious quivering palm trees and emerald seas. And yet, one of the first shots of Tahiti shows a large sign above a shop that speaks for itself: "Tahiti Quincaillerie" (Tahiti Hardware).

This uninterrupted passage that drives the entire film takes place under the sign of the *traversal*: Trébor traverses a lake swimming, traverses mountains on his bike, meticulously cares for his tires; borders are traversed, passports are burned, a stretch of snow is traversed by a body cruelly dragged by horses; oceans are traversed, an inlet is forded; until, finally, a sled pulled by vigorously whipped dogs ends the film by leading off into the depth of the screen. And in the hysterical laughter of the dogsled driver there is an echo of the explosion of ribbons at the naval baptism, the joyous and troubling promise of an ever-renewing departure that returns, in counterpoint, to a shot of a beautiful copper propeller, motionless and half-submerged. If there is a film that knows how not to end, this is it.

This permanent circulation, this *perpetuum mobile*, also entails very few interiors amid the profusion of broadly open exteriors: hills, roads, coasts, open sea. The interiors are often seen from outside (through windows, both the young couple's and Henri's, that echo each other from the beginning to the end of the film), or they are precarious (cabin, hut, hotel room, nondescript offices). Everything is outdoors; everything is turned toward the outdoors, one might say, recalling that *tourner* also means to shoot a film. The relation between interiority and exteriority (that of space, of the foreigner) is determined as an exposure of the former to the latter and vice versa: In fact, interiority is reduced to a supposition and is never clearly presented or accessible. Who is Trébor? Who is Toni? Henri? And so on . . . We understand that this is not the question, or, rather, it's the question that does not lead to any answer, that wants to be pursued indefinitely.

Gauguin, in these Marquesas Islands, made his great painting *Where Do We Come From? What Are We? Where*

Are We Going? If there is a painting that resembles a film—and in Cinemascope—this is it.

VI

The uninterrupted passage takes place in double company: that of women and that of dogs, the former linked to the latter in the figures of the customs officer, the wild girl, the Russian woman, and the dog breeder (who is credited as "The Queen of the Northern Hemisphere").

The women don't travel, or at least they aren't filmed traveling, except in a sovereign fashion (the "queen" takes her sleigh, the Russian her horse). They are not caught up in the wanderings of men. Instead they watch over places—the pharmacist her pharmacy, even while she makes visits to the hermit in the forest; the dog breeder her breeding grounds; the Tahitian mother her house and her children—or they provide care (the pharmacist, the masseuse). And if they do wander, which is the case with the wild girl and the Russian, then it's only as doublets of the wandering Trébor: The former is in a sense his female double; she also takes refuge in the forest, though we don't learn why; the latter is the nemesis who tracks his every step. Trébor exists, in a way, only as a figure doubled from each side by these two allegories of himself.

Apart from Trébor, the wild girl is the only person to be shown almost entirely naked and in a state of pleasure—him in the sun, her in the bath (which she takes at Trébor's house, in his tub, in his absence), and it is her heart that, in a dream or hallucination, is seen torn out and sniffed by dogs, while another image (of blood and dog hair on a bracelet) convinces us that she has been killed or wounded. It is suggested, not explicitly, by the parallel between their bodies infatuated with themselves as though with "nature," that she is one of

Trébor's feminine souls, namely, his body, his pleasure. The Russian is the other part of his femininity: his conscience, his guilt, the voice of his soul—not necessarily a moral soul but one heavy with memory, with vigilance and cunning calculation. The wild girl does not speak (unless she is the one whispering during the opening credits, in obscure language that includes mention of "giving a heart"—but it could be someone else; I will return to this). The Russian, however, does speak, in a sharp, lacerating manner, or she sends electronic messages. She tortures Trébor as well as his son, while the wild girl—in reality or in a dream—is herself tortured. While the Russian declares that Trébor's heart is "empty," the wild girl, perhaps, hoped for nothing more than to share her heart with him.

Two women are caretakers. The village pharmacist, who is shown performing her function as a way to emphasize this, brings Trébor his medication at the same time she comes to share his bed and to pass along the edge of his disquiet. The blind Korean masseuse visits Trébor in his hotel, climbs onto the bed to massage him. The multifaceted contrast between these two women says something about their two forms of medicine and their two worlds. The passage from one to the other is also the passage from one life to another, and before that from one hemisphere to another. But Trébor will not abandon Western medicine; he will continue to take his (new) meds, and he will return to the hospital (if we can say "return," since we saw nothing of the first hospital or of the transplant). In this new hospital, in Papeete, he is observed by two nurses with sweet and young faces whose expressions betray both tenderness and something like a worried interest in this sick man, who must be exceptional here. But their faces also signify, in this brief distraction from their medical tasks, that medicine is not the point here . . .

Heart sickness is the province of the man; the treatment—if not cure, which may be impossible—and care is the province of women. But at the same time, their doubling signifies that it has less to do with medical technique than with the impossible "technique" of a true change of heart, of an interior metamorphosis for Trébor, of the conversion or revelation that the "beloved son" might represent. Because all the love of which he is capable is tied up in this "beloved"—all this love that might after all be nothing, or nothing but these very words, nothing but this nearly silent incantation.

Two of the women are mothers—the customs officer and the Marquesan. Both of them are doomed by Trébor to suffer in their motherhood: His impossible paternity is the double of their wounded maternity. The other women are childless: He is their child, under their care or even under their surveillance, under their gaze—troubled, attentive, or distant; mocking or even blind and consequently able to see straight into his heart.

What is the affinity shared by the dogs and the women? The presentiment of intrusion. The dog trained by the customs officer knows how to sniff out illicit merchandise, the Russian's dogs know how to track Trébor the same way his own dogs intuit strange approaches in the night, and the breeder's dogs excitedly sense the approach of Trébor's. His dogs (which are, not accidentally, females), once he abandons them because the breeder refuses to watch them (surely sensing his imminent flight), lose no time finding the wild girl and the body or bodies beneath the ice. At the end, when Toni approaches a house to which someone has directed him, where he will learn the truth, it is one of the Russian's dogs that barks—the ones that keep close to her when, from afar, she observes people exiting the morgue.

Dogs are at the intersection of the natural and the foreign. Trébor, lying nude in the sun, curls up with one of his dogs like he would with a woman, and when his lover comes to see him she caresses his dogs with affection. The dogs are something like a pure state of affect, but this affect is also what puts them on alert, whether in the night when a prowler approaches or on the frozen expanse when the ice is hiding a corpse. While Trébor warms himself in the sun, one of the dogs intuits the presence of someone whose silhouette then appears between the trees.

The kinship between dogs and women intensifies in the well-appointed carriage the breeder drives—amid loud snaps of the whip and cries of encouragement—with alacrity through the snowy forest. It speeds ahead toward other strangenesses, toward other possible intrusions; it speeds ahead, the ultimate irony of fate and the undecidability of pathways and passages resounding in the driver's manic laughter, which also betrays the jubilation of a director who has cast her film in lavish splendor toward the depths of her own strangeness.

The obscurity of the closing shot resembles that of the opening, and this is the moment to hear again the woman with a barely audible voice—and a face one can only guess at—whispering over the credits. Among the words and phrases we think we discern are "I hear you" and "give a heart." Is this woman the Russian? Nothing is confirmed. But it could be that the ultimate ambiguity, the enigma of intrusion, is at play here in a strange relation of love between this avenger and her sworn enemy.

But this secret, like all the others, this real or merely simulated secret—simulated between characters whose relationships with one another will never be clearly established and simulated by the filmmaker for us (the relation between her and us is also very unclear)—is carried off, along with the whole film, by the most secret one of all, the woman who trusts in nothing but the furious running of her dogs.

May 4, 2005
—*Translated by Anna Moschovakis*

Notes

Foreword

This Foreword is adapted from an introduction to *The Intruder* given at Metrograph NYC.

1. [Nancy offers a different version of the origin of the text. See p. 80.—Trans.]

Introduction

1. For an illuminating discussion of both book and film, see Martine Beugnet, "The Practice of Strangeness: *L'intrus*, from Jean-Luc Nancy (2000) to Claire Denis (2004)," in *The Essay Film: Dialogue, Politics, Utopia*, ed. Elizabeth A. Papazian and Caroline Eades (London: Wallflower, 2016).
2. Beugnet, "The Practice of Strangeness," 71.
3. Beugnet, "The Practice of Strangeness," 80.
4. *Le reflux* is the only film Gégauff made. Loosely adapted from *The Ebb-Tide* (1894), by Robert Louis Stevenson and his stepson Lloyd Osborne, it was never released but was screened in 2022 at MoMA in New York (see https://www.moma.org/calendar/events/7843). It's worth noting that Denis is not the only

filmmaker to claim inspiration from Nancy's text. Nicolas Klotz and Elisabeth Perceval have also cited it as a point of departure for their film *La blessure/The Wound* (2004), which focuses much more directly on issues around immigration into France, refugees seeking asylum, and the violent policing of international borders in a postcolonial world.

The Intruder

This text was first published in response to an invitation by Abdelwahab Meddeb to participate, for his review *Dédale*, in a number that he entitled "La venue de l'étranger" (The advent of the stranger), no. 9–10 (Paris: Maisonneuve and Larose, 1999). [This translation first appeared in Jean-Luc Nancy, *Corpus* (New York: Fordham University Press, 2008). It appears here in lightly revised form. The postscripts appear here in English for the first time.] The epigraph is from Antonin Artaud, in *84*, no. 5–6 (1948): 103.

1. [In French *l'étranger* can mean both stranger and foreigner; likewise (as here) *l'étrangeté* can mean strangeness or foreignness.—Trans.]

2. [In English in original.—Trans.]

3. I rejoin certain thoughts of friends: Alex speaking in German about being *un-eins* with AIDS, to speak of an existence whose unity lies in division and discord with itself, or Giorgio speaking in Greek about a *bios* that is only *zóé*, about a form of life that would be no more than merely maintained. See Alex Garcia-Düttmann, *At Odds with AIDS*, trans. Peter Gilgen and Conrad Scott-Curtis (Stanford, CA: Stanford University Press, 1996); and Giorgio Agamben, *Homo Sacer: Sovereign Power and Bare Life*, trans. Daniel Heller-Roazen (Stanford, CA: Stanford University Press, 1998). To say nothing of Derrida's grafts, supplements, and prostheses. And the memory of a drawing by Sylvie Blocher, *Jean-Luc with the Heart of a Woman*.

4. [Nancy is evoking here the choral ode in Sophocles's *Antigone*, to which Heidegger devoted a lengthy commentary in his 1942 lecture course *Hölderlin's Hymn "The Ister." The*

Ister is also the name of a documentary film from 2004 by David Barison and Daniel Ross in which Nancy is interviewed, along with Bernard Stiegler, Philippe Lacoue-Labarthe, and Hans-Jürgen Syberberg.—Trans.]

5. [The past participles Nancy uses here to describe his body are "arrangé, bricolé, appareillé," words all with multiple meanings. The meanings of the verb *appareiller* go in several directions, indicating a pairing or matching together (based on *pareil*, same), the attachment of an artificial limb, the more general implication of an apparatus or instrument (*appareil*), the preparations for a complex technical process, and (as a specific instance of the latter) casting off from a port or an anchoring point. This last sense is suggested again at the beginning of postscript 3, in the title of the "note" quoted there, where the phrase "au long cours" means "long-term" but also evokes distant ocean travel—and with it both masterful sailing and a kind of unmoored drifting with no visible end . . .—Trans.]

The Intruder According to Claire Denis

This essay was first published as Jean-Luc Nancy, "*The Intruder* According to Claire Denis," trans. Anna Moschovakis, in *The Films of Claire Denis: Intimacy on the Border*, ed. Marjorie Vecchio (London: I. B. Tauris, 2014). It is used by permission of Bloomsbury Publishing Plc. The version appearing here has been lightly edited.

Jean-Luc Nancy (1940–2021) was Distinguished Professor of Philosophy at the Universite Marc Bloch, Strasbourg and one of the late twentieth and early twenty-first century's foremost thinkers of politics, art, and the body. His wide-ranging thought runs through many books, including *Being Singular Plural, The Ground of the Image, Corpus, The Disavowed Community,* and *Sexistence.*

Jeff Fort is Associate Professor of French and Francophone Studies at the University of California, Davis. He is the author of *The Imperative to Write* (2014) and translator of more than a dozen books, by Jean Genet, Jacques Derrida, Maurice Blanchot, Jean-Luc Nancy, and others.

Claire Denis is the director of fifteen films, including *Beau Travail, Chocolat, 35 Shots of Rum, White Material,* and *High Life*. Her most recent film, *Stars at Noon*, won the Grand Prix at the Cannes Film Festival.

www.ingramcontent.com/pod-product-compliance
Lightning Source LLC
Chambersburg PA
CBHW060502080526
44584CB00015B/1518